The Worldview Series

Thoughts that Give Me Life

ALI NAJI

THE MAINSTAY
FOUNDATION

By: The Mainstay Foundation

© 2018 The Mainstay Foundation

ALL RIGHTS RESERVED. No part of this work covered by the copyright may be reproduced or used in any form or by any means – graphic, electronic, or mechanical, including photocopying, recording, taping, web distribution, information storage and retrieval systems, or in any other manner – without the written permission of the Mainstay Foundation.

Printed in the United States.

ISBN: 978-1943393374

In the name of *what is true*, including *what is right*, I offer the following attempt to the *guardian* behind the scenes and to the network of noble souls shining in recognition of *the one with no need*.

CONTENTS

Contents 1
Thoughts that Give Me Life 3
   Acknowledgements 5
   Thoughts that Give Me Life 7
   Need for no Need... 9
      Look to the Sun 9
      Realize your Potential..10
      See Excellence in Different Colors..............................13
   The Right Thing to Do 15
   Guidance to Achieve my Purpose..21
   Guardianship behind the Scenes...27
   What Goes Around Comes Around...31
Notes...35

THOUGHTS THAT GIVE ME LIFE

Acknowledgements

In writing this short booklet, I considered including references to expert thinkers with relevant discussions branching off of the core ideas I invite the reader to reflect on. But I decided that doing so would likely defeat the purpose of this publication. As a conscious reader will notice, although I discuss ideas that can be examined more closely by experts, I intently attempt to elucidate them in a way accessible to the non-expert.

Nevertheless, I realize the significance of being self-aware regarding the influence of multiple factors on my use of language, terms, categories and frameworks.[1] Although truth is out there for any sincere seeker, we seldom journey in a vacuum. For the ensuing reflections, I am thus indebted to various gracious souls, communities, and environments. First and foremost, I thank the truth for being there in a way that is accessible to some extent, regardless of all else. I thank my loving parents, supportive family and reliable friends, especially my beloved wife. I am forever grateful to my mentors and educators. Institutions and communities of learning across time and space command my lasting gratitude and reverence. I extend special appreciation to the Mainstay Foundation and its editorial team for supporting this project. To those I have neglected proper recognition and thanks, I cannot truly do you justice. As the wise have said, "How can I truly thank you when being able to say, 'thank you,' calls for another, 'thank you'?"[2] Any good in my work is yours and the shortcomings are all my own.

Thoughts that Give Me Life

The following thoughts are packed with life. But it is up to the reader to see for her/himself. If I could have pinpointed any thoughts more pivotal to my own life than these, I would have. Almost every, if not every, sentence in this short booklet addresses a condensed facet of discussion regarding one of these five key ideas. A reader unfamiliar with these discourses might not recognize it, but can rest assured that there are long conversations in between the lines. That being said, I have avoided technical and even traditional terms, and have instead attempted to cast these timeless truths in a language more akin to our times. My humble attempt has been to move from point to point in an intelligible fashion, while inviting a contemplative type of reading.

Need for no Need

Look to the Sun

When the sun rises every morning, how often do we think about it as anything more than just that? Okay, so it rises. There are interesting colors that decorate the horizon in the process. Anything else? Maybe the reader has something else in mind. But consider this thought if you haven't already. Do we *see* the Sun or do we *see* rays of light? The rays of light travel at (or close to) the speed of light, traversing the distance between the Sun and our planet Earth, until we are able to see them. The rays are bright, warm and beaming in many directions. For some reason, however, we realize that the rays don't have what it takes to explain their own power. They project toward us and rain down upon us, scattering their sprinkles of light all around. But aren't they in need of an explanation beyond themselves? What is the source of this heat, this light? The blazing Sun. Whether the rays light up our skies for part of a day, a week, or a million years, it is just the same. Ask the rays of light, "How long have you been around?" In their own way, they might as well be whispering, "We don't remember. Why does it matter?" *The rays are still limited by, and thus in need, of something beyond themselves. They are not powerful enough to explain their own power. The rays can enchant us and even blind us, but they still stand in utter need of the Sun.*

Realize your Potential

What keeps me from realizing my potential as an individual? Is it the fact that I have needs and limitations? But the rays of light are limited too! Still, they are luminous and brighten up the skies for everyone in their path. Their power issues forth from the Sun. The rays "tell" us their story in their own way. They do not have to use words for us to "hear" what they are saying. They simply shine and make us wonder, "What is their secret?" *If they could speak, maybe they would give us a hint, "We are in need of the one with no need."* The connection to their source turns their limits into distinction, gives them their sparkle and, indeed, their very existence. The more profoundly we sense our own sun, the more our thoughts line up with that connection, our limits can become distinctions and we can shine toward our potential. The secret can be ours as well. When our thoughts spring forth in that spirit, our needs can remind us of our true source of beauty, make us unique, and draw attention to our deepest secret - the brightest sun.

I suspect that the reader has figured it out already. The Sun of our solar system, as powerful as it may be, does not escape the equation laid out above. No matter how long it has been lit, and regardless of the duration it remains kindled, the Sun is in need of an explanation beyond itself as well. It is not self-explanatory. As hot as it may be…as luminous as we can see…the Sun has limits in various ways.

Time, space, energy, awareness and life are things which the Sun is limited by, is in need of, or is deficient in. As proud as the Sun appears to us and as potent as it may seem, it has no choice but to testify (in its own way), "I am in need of the one with no need." *The one with no need* is the treasure everyone and everything is hiding. *The one with no need* has no lack, no deficiency, no limitation. No one can have an excellence that *the one with no need* lacks. Otherwise, there would be some limit, some relative weakness, some need in *the one with no need*! So there can only be *one* with no need. *The one with no need* is so infinitely unique. There is *no room* for another with no need. Every *other* is in need – in the shadow of *the one with no need*. No rays and no shadows can exist without that ultimate source of light. The inherent light of *the one with no need* is the self-explanatory explanation for all other illumination. Every other being can only come onto the scene of reality through the light of *the one with no need*. Do we sense that warmth and light? Do we feel the power of life?

See Excellence in Different Colors

The *one with no need* encompasses every possible dimension, owns all life forms, and has pervasive perception. Every color of excellence is like a window pane through which we can attempt to see the *one with no need*. Through the window of power, we see *the one with no need* as the almighty. Through the window of life, we see *the one with no need* as absolute life. The window of awareness shows us the all-knowing. *The one with no need* is all of these at once. *These are windows for us to understand – not composing parts, separate entities, or changing roles.* The secret is hidden because the source of light is so bright. Rays of light are what we see, but it is the Sun that allows them to be. *The one with no need* is the truest light of existence, the source of all brilliance... How can such light be hidden? Hidden like the water to the fish at sea... Hidden like the air that allows us to be... The hidden? Or the apparent? The inner? Or the outer? Call *the one with no need* what you may, in word or phrase, for to *the one with no need* belong all beautiful names.

The Right Thing to Do

Some say that instinct drives us to do what we do. Sure, our upbringing has a role to play. So does social pressure and expectation. But break it down and there is nothing but biological programming, plain and simple – so some would say. Why does a mother stay up worried about her baby? Why does a young child help a helpless old lady? Why does a thief despise theft when [s]he is the victim? Why does a liar hate it when someone lies to her/him? Is everything about dollars and cents to us or is there something much deeper? Do I only love someone if there is something I will get in return?

Do I condemn the murder of distant innocents or is it not my concern? Am I willing to give my time, wealth and life for something greater, or do I die on the inside as I say, "maybe later"? Isn't injustice wrong no matter the location? Isn't thanking kindness with kindness the befitting reaction? Am I a greedy merchant seeking material gains in every situation or does my knowledge that I am doing *the right thing* give me enough satisfaction?

Sure, I may instinctively want to survive. I may naturally struggle to protect myself and my own. But there is more to my choices than that. I am no robot. Sometimes bad habits might get the best of me. I may become prey to my own instinctive tendency. But I have a choice. I formed my habits, once upon a time, through repeated choices and actions. I sense my instinct and I also sense my ability to think about other things, weigh my options and decide. I realize that there is more to my choices than material gains and losses. Why should I act in light of this instinct or that feeling? Why should I think it through and be careful in my reasoning? Because it is *the right thing to do*. Deep down, I know – as clearly as I can see the sun – that some decisions are lost and others are won. *Decision-making does not only yield material fortunes and financial poverty. Making a choice reveals either moral riches or moral bankruptcy*. Moral "instincts" – if we can call them that – are distinct in at least two ways: (1) moral "instincts" drive us to maintain *moral* life, not only *biological* life; and (2) moral "instincts" are matched by *knowledge* that some choices (*the right things to do*) simply "fit" with *what is complete and excellent in reality*. At the foundational level, this self-evident knowledge is a mirror reflecting reality. Upbringing, education, and physical factors can only distort so much. A mirror is a mirror, regardless where it was made. Just as I know the mathematical basics like 1+1=2, I also know the moral basics about *the right thing to do*. Beyond the basics, as things require further calculation, however, I may need help...

The one with no need knows everything about *the right thing to do* and has all the power to do it. There is no limit/deficiency/need holding back *the one with no need's* endless spring of life. I must recognize, then, that all actions of *the one with no need* have been, are and always will be *the right thing to do*. Sometimes I understand those actions and at other times my knowledge is too limited to encompass all the variables at stake. Why make the snake in a way to have poisonous venom? Well, the venom may harm me but it protects the snake! Why create a world with earthquakes, volcanoes and other natural "disasters"? Perhaps there *are* other worlds without such occurrences... But in *this* world, it must be that this is the best *overall* system – even if we do not understand all the details involved.

The one with no need powers us up with our choice-making freedom every passing moment. To grant us the opportunity to make our own choices, paint our true colors, and soar toward our potential – all of that is great... To be free – to be more than a rock or a tree. We *can choose* to be the people of conscience, the heroes, and the cream of the crop. But, as we know, some of us abuse our freedom, make the wrong choices and silence our inner voice of integrity. *The one with no need* is the power needed by the entire system constantly, but the choices we make within the system are our own responsibility. Light belongs to the glorious sun, while darkness is the property of the shadows. Any right choice we make is thanks to *the one with no need* and every evil decision we make is our own deed.

Guidance to Achieve my Purpose

Why must I have a purpose in my actions? Is it simply because I have something to gain? If I have a need to fulfill then I act with that purpose in mind or at heart. But even if all my typical needs were satisfied one day, wouldn't *acting with purpose* still be *the right thing to do*? *Acting with purpose* is wise and acting wisely is *the right thing to do*. The woman who has it all may still calculate her every move, not because she worries about a need to fulfill, but because she knows that being purposeful is *the right thing to do*.

Providing for the needy is a noble gesture. But what's in it for me? There could be a lot in it for me. Maybe I give only in hopes that one day someone will give me. Or maybe I give in order to get recognition… Good or bad, there could be many motives driving my choice. But can't I give the needy simply because it is *the right thing to do*? *The right thing to do* is a worthy pursuit on its own merit, regardless whether I have something to gain or not. Supporting the weak, defending the oppressed, feeding the hungry, and helping those who have lost their way are all examples of *the right thing to do*.

The one with no need has nothing to gain. Yet, acting aimlessly is not *the right thing to do*. There must, then, be a purpose in the actions of *the one with no need*. Is it for *personal* gain? That cannot be the case – *the one with no need* has no needs to fulfill, nothing to gain! Then it must be in order for *others* to gain, for *others* to achieve, for *others* to excel. Thus, the wisest purpose resides in having *others* be the best that they can be. But why? Why choose to shine? Why have the spring of life flow? Why be so generous? Why have such initiative? If we listen closely, we might hear the answer in the cries of the weak, the needy, the poor and the oppressed, "Give us because you are powerful and we are in need. Show us your mercy because you can. Bring us out of the darkness because you are the light. It is *the right thing to do*. If anyone were to do it, it would be you."

How do I achieve my purpose? How can I reach my potential? Where do I start? I should begin with what I already *do* know. Doing the right thing includes believing what is true, rejecting what is false, being open-minded on things I am not sure of yet, and leading a moral life. What next though? Don't I expect *the one with no need* to provide me a more comprehensive plan? What do I do with all the complicated questions in between? How do I manage to be *the best I can be* when my information is deficient, my roadmap is incomplete and I have no navigation system?! To leave me without holistic guidance would be unbefitting of *the one with no need*. So I anticipate that *the one with no need* will make a *flawless* roadmap available to me, either: (1) directly (if my personal "receiver" can handle it!), or (2) indirectly.

Without *direct* access to the full-fledged navigation system, I am left with the hopes of finding *indirect* access – that is through someone who *I can prove* had direct access. If I do not have a GPS, then I can ride with someone who does. I am in search for something more than an ordinary GPS, however. I am looking for a walking, talking beacon of guidance. I am anticipating a *role model* in *free* choice-making, not a robotic machine. Someone *like* me, but not like *me*. Someone that I can relate to – someone who feels, who thinks, who faces challenges, and who makes choices… But different than me, better than me – someone who has *always* made commendable decisions, who has *never* lost touch with the ultimate sun and who has what it takes to be a *chosen one*. Such a soul would choose to act *either reasonably or better*. Still, a *chosen one* would feel the guilt of "failing" to be greater… *In relation to the greatest sun, the first place has already been won*. A *chosen one* would be a lighthouse in word and in deed – sent forth by the sun of existence, *the one with no need*.

How will we know when we have found a *chosen one*? We will *know*. Evidence... proof... that is how. The words of a *chosen one* would be sound, reasonable and consistent with the words of every other established *chosen one*. A *chosen one* would be in sync with what is right. Such a messenger would not claim to be more than a link to the ultimate sun. We can expect this noble soul to have been known as a trustworthy and honest one. A tree is known by its fruits. The impact of a supposed *chosen one* on the quality (if not also the quantity) of upright apprentices can give an indication that this particular claimant is something special. But the decisive proof is when the sun of existence gives the stamp of approval to a *chosen one*... For if a moral individual, in that critical position, can introduce a *miracle* then it must be by that sun's permission. If all the facts seem to indicate that this potential *chosen one* would not tell a lie, then *the one with no need* would not fool us by giving a liar another alibi. Allowing a liar to produce a supernatural feat *beyond human-expert reproduction*, would not be *the right thing to do* and would surely be unbefitting of *the one with no need's* perfection. For example, can the eligible claimant split the sea, raise the dead, or recite eloquence beyond comparison? If so, then herein resides decisive proof of *the one with no need's* approval and a *chosen one's* truthful position.

Guardianship behind the Scenes

I no longer operate with the basic form of moral life, I have something more. My heart beats with a yearning for an unnamed *chosen one*. I want my choices to push me in the direction of excellence on every level. The reader probably realizes that there have been many *chosen ones* throughout the ages. A *chosen one* comes with the "software" suitable for humanity's "operating system". As humans change, the software might be "updated" at the hands of the next *chosen one*. But what about the time in between? What happens after a *chosen one* has lived, delivered a message and then departed? Better yet, what if the final update has already been delivered? What if the deal has been *sealed* and the last *chosen one* has come and gone? Who guards the most recent software from viruses and other threats? Who is responsible for maintaining, at least, *the bare minimum* integrity of the program, the prescription, the *chosen one*'s legacy? Who is the succeeding *guardian*, the moral compass, and the appointed deputy?

There must be *at least* one active, living, *guardian*. There must be a qualified, *living* point of communication with *the one with no need*. This is not a "*chosen one's* communication," but the connection for a *guardian's* function... For one who lives up to the standard, and readily steps in if ordered. *The one with no need* is the light, the supreme commander. A *chosen one* embodies that will as a messenger. A *guardian* is impeccable, similar to a *chosen one*, but not the same. While not introducing *new* "*chosen-one* software," a *guardian* lives up to the name. *Protecting* the message, *keeping* the fort and *being ready* to intervene... These are some roles of a *guardian* even when that *guardian* goes *unseen*. This is regardless whether the *guardian* is someone we know, or a *hidden* master behind the scenes who lives *incognito*. Just as I anticipate the presence of a *chosen one* at some point in history, I also expect a *guardian* – after the final *chosen one* – for every century. Before a *guardian's* demise, *the one with no need* would either choose another; or prolong the living *guardian*'s life, for some wisdom, beyond any other. A *chosen one* would make the coming *guardian* known and the next *guardian* would as well. A true *guardian* would have profound moral character and unrivaled knowledge to tell. Impeccability behind closed doors is a secret known only through the Divine, so the immaculate *guardian* would be appointed with a Divine word or sign. *The one with no need* brings the universe to fruition through guidance protected... Such protection in the physical world is through the *guardian* manifested. Without that mainstay, the universe would go under... In peril without the one to fulfill its wonder.

Providing a *guardian* is in tune with the excellence of *the one with no need*. Furthermore, a *guardian* would *choose* to be *prepared*, night and day, and would not misread. A model leader, arbiter, and virtue-promoter – a *guardian* is the critical justice protector. But if other people abuse their freedom and choose to be *unprepared*, their injustice can deprive us from a *guardian* publicly declared. *The one with no need* offers us the moral link, but – from that pure river – does not *force* us to drink. If wrongdoers reject a *guardian*'s public leadership, then a *guardian* might act only behind the scenes. The *guardian* would resort to a plan B, organize a "shadow authority" of sorts – consider what that means. This would be the toll of people's freedom to choose – sometimes we would win and at others we would lose. Yet, the existence of a living *guardian* would *guarantee* the *threshold* of guidance protected. There is an elaborate network of moral navigation, a hub rigorously defended. The *extinct* schools of thinking and practice thus become irrelevant. The *guarded community* persists through every crucial incident. By process of elimination, truth is evident. Which network struggles for this *guardian* every moment? *The right-hand men and women* of the *guardian* may not be flawless, but they breathe the life of these thoughts, are well-aware and are not lawless.

What Goes Around Comes Around

Our new life is waiting for us – there is so much to achieve. Excellence can be our destiny if progress is our company. I may not be able to be the *best* overnight but I can try to get *better* every moment! Every choice counts. We are linked to a network of life that spans time and space. Isn't it time to start acting like it? My actions have ripple effects and I may not know how far the ripples go – they could go on and on without end, for all I know! Good or bad, right or wrong, what I choose to do – *at heart and with my limbs* - matters. *The one with no need* would not shine us into existence simply to be obliterated in a few cosmic years. That could not be because what, then, would be the point? Rather, *the one with no need* has a purpose for us – to journey toward endless excellence. Doing *the right thing* matters because my choices can make their mark on that infinity. I think the reader sees where I am going with this.

But the matter is actually far closer to home than the thought of eternity. *The one with no need* always does *the right thing*: no act of kindness should go unrewarded. The deeper the sincerity, devotion and impact, the greater the anticipated recognition would be. If that universal "reply" to our kind messages does not happen in this world, then it must become a reality in some other realm. Even if a partial "response" is felt in this world, we can expect a complete response in a world beyond this one. What about our unanswered prayers? In the hands of *the one with no need*, all is recorded.

Every act of evil *deserves* to be punished. The record must be set straight. Criminals and terrorists must face justice for that which they have done.

The victims have a right to compensation now and in the long run. The forces of the dark side have killed the innocent with cold blood and the past cannot be undone. Therefore, there is another world *in which all stand for trial* and the innocent have already won. Some say, "*What goes around comes around.*" Well, it *should*, anyway. I can see without a doubt: the reward of kindness is kindness – that is here to stay. The *evil* that goes around *should* come around too, *unless one can make amends some way*. Nevertheless, if a lost soul has managed not to break the "mercy-receiver" beyond repair, then picking up the endless "broadcast of mercy" is possible for someone who does not despair.

Our light is but a reminder of the ultimate sun. Will we shine with an awareness of our truest secret? Will our actions play the tones of *the right thing to do*? Will we search for answers and stand for what is true? *Chosen one* after *chosen one,* and *guardian* after *guardian*, *the one with no need* has appointed our mainstay. Now it is up to us to breathe with new life, to reject all injustice, to uphold every honor and *to do as we say*.

NOTES

[1] References are particularly due to lectures and works by:

- S. Muḥammad Ḥusayn al-Ṭabāṭabā'ī
- Sh. Murtaḍá al-Muṭahharī
- S. Muḥammad Bāqir al-Ṣadr
- Sh. Ghulām Riḍā al-Fayyāḍī
- Sh. Nāṣir Makārim al-Shīrāzī
- Sh. Ja'far al-Subḥānī
- S. Ja'far al-Ḥakīm
- S. Munīr al-Khabbāz
- S. Muḥammad Bāqir al-Sīstānī
- S. Muḥammad 'Alī Baḥr al-'ulūm
- S. Sāmī al-Badrī

- S. Muḥammad Rizvī

[2] Attributed to ʿAlī ibn al-Ḥusayn, known as Zayn al-ʿābidīn, Munājāt al-Shākirīn

www.ingramcontent.com/pod-product-compliance
Lightning Source LLC
Chambersburg PA
CBHW022347040426
42449CB00006B/767